Crochet Shawl Patterns

Easy and Stylish Crochet Shawls

Melissa Hammock

Copyright © 2020 **Melissa Hammock**

All rights reserved.

ISBN: 9798672855349

DEDICATION

The author and publisher have provided this e-book to you for your personal use only. You may not make this e-book publicly available in any way. Copyright infringement is against the law. If you believe the copy of this e-book you are reading infringes on the author's copyright, please notify the publisher at: https://us.macmillan.com/piracy

Contents

Easy Scrap Yarn Shawl 1

Juliette Shawl 4

Autumn Leaves Filet Crochet Shawl 17

Any Season Asymmetrical Shawlette 21

My Story Shawl 24

Halo Shawl 30

Winter Shawl 36

Pop Of Color Shawl 41

April Showers Shawl 45

Crochet Triangle Shawl 52

Spring Shawl 57

Crochet Shawl Patterns

Easy Scrap Yarn Shawl

Crochet Abbreviations Used in Recipe

Here are the crochet stitches and abbreviations used throughout this shawl pattern:

* = a repeat in the pattern

[ ] = repeat instructions within brackets as many times as indicated

ch = chain

hdc = half double crochet

inc(d) = increase(d)

st(s) = stitch(es)

Pattern

Ch 4 loosely, 2 hdc in 2nd ch from hook, 2 hdc in each of the next 2 ch sts -- 6 hdc.

Row 1: Ch 1, 2 hdc in 1st st, 1 hdc in next st, [2 hdc in next st] twice, hdc in next st, 2 hdc in last st -- 10 hdc.

Row 2: Ch 1, 2 hdc in 1st st, hdc in next 3 sts, [2 hdc in next st] twice, hdc in next 3 sts, 2 hdc in last st -- 14 hdc.

Place locking stitch markers on the center 2 sts. To do this begin counting at one edge and place marker on the 7th and 8th hdc st.

Row 3: Ch 1, 2 hdc in 1st st, hdc in next 5 sts, [2 hdc in next st with stitch marker, replace marker on last st made] twice, hdc in next 5 sts, 2 hdc in last st -- 18 hdc.

Row 4: Ch 1, 2 hdc in first st, hdc in each st to marker, [2 hdc in next st with stitch marker, replace marker on last st made] twice, hdc in each st to last st, 2 hdc in last st -- 4 sts inc'd.

*Continue working Row 4 until shawl has reached the desired measurements. Be careful to place the stitch markers on the second of each increased stitch or the center point will begin to veer off in the wrong direction.

Finishing: Fasten off and weave in any ends.

Crochet Shawl Patterns

Juliette Shawl

Materials

Size:

23" long

Yarn:

Cascade Yarns Whirligig: (60% Superwash Merino Wool / 20% Nylon / 20% Acrylic), Size 3 (11 wpi DK weight), 546 yds / 200 g (yds/g = 2.73)

Reds 04 – 1 skein, (410 yds / 150 g)

-or-

Frabjous Fibers Mad Hatter Mini Skein pack:

33 Lime to Turquoise Shadow (Color Morphs)

Hook:

US – 7, 4.5 mm

Gauge:

18 sts x 9 rows = 4" [10 cm] in double crochet

Other supplies:

yarn needle

removable stitch markers

Stitches and Abbreviations: click on highlighted sts for tutorials

ch – chain

dc – double crochet

sc – single crochet

sl st – slip stitch

sp(s) – space(s)

st(s) – stitch(es)

Pattern

Rnd/Row counts are at the end of each row in {braces}, if the count has changed from the previous Rnd/Row.

The marked ch-2 is the center point of the shawl, and separates the 2 sides of the shawl.

Chs and sl sts are not included in Round/Row counts unless specified.

When a marker is placed after a ch 2, it should be placed around the ch 2 space just made.

When a marker is placed a st is made, it should be placed around the loop on the hook.

When a marker is placed on a st made in the past, it should be placed around both loops of the top of the st.

Pattern:

Set Up Rnd: Fdc 86, slip st to top of first fdc to form a loop, stitch bottom of loop seam shut with tail and weave in end. {86 sts}

Crochet Shawl Patterns

Row 1: Pm 2 sts to the right of hook, ch 1, skip 1 (dc, ch 1, dc, ch 2, pm, dc, ch 1, dc) in next st, ch 1, skip 1, sl st in each of next 3 sts, skip 1, pm. {2 dc on each side}

Row 2: Ch 1, turn, dc in first ch-1 sp, (dc, ch 1, dc) in next ch-1 sp, rm, (dc, ch 1, dc, ch 2, pm, dc, ch 1, dc) in ch-2 sp, (dc, ch 1, dc) in

next ch-1 sp, dc in last ch-1 sp, ch 1, sl st in marked st, rm, sl st in each of next 2 sts, skip 1, pm. {5 dc on each side}

Row 3: Ch 1, turn, (dc, ch 1, dc) in each of next 3 ch-1 sps, rm, (dc, ch 1, dc, ch 2, pm, dc, ch 1, dc) in ch-2 sp, (dc, ch 1, dc) in each of next 3 ch-1 sps, ch 1, sl st in marked st, rm, sl st in each of next 2 sts, skip 1, pm. {8 dc on each side}

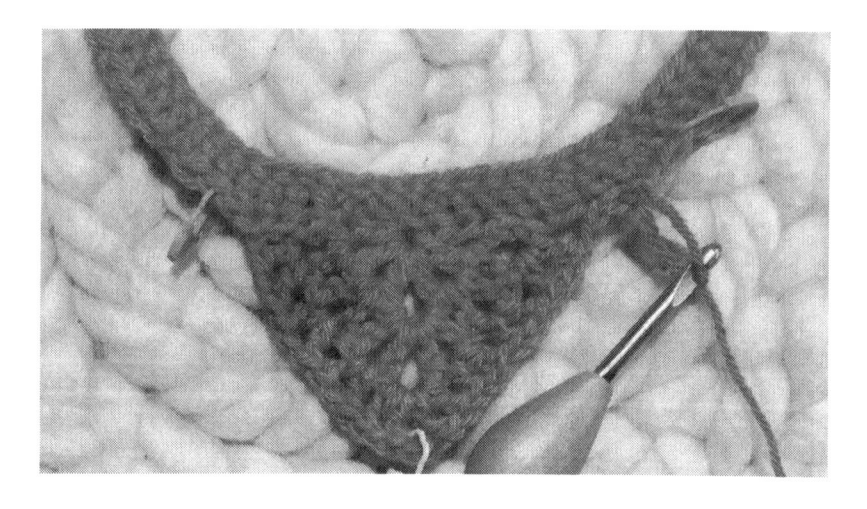

Row 4: Ch 1, turn, dc in first ch-1 sp, (dc, ch 1, dc) in next 4 ch-1 sps, rm, (dc, ch 1, dc, ch 2, pm, dc, ch 1, dc) in ch-2 sp, (dc, ch 1, dc) in each of next 4 ch-1 sps, dc in last ch-1 sp, ch 1, sl st in marked st, rm, sl st in each of next 2 sts, skip 1, pm. {11 dc on each side}

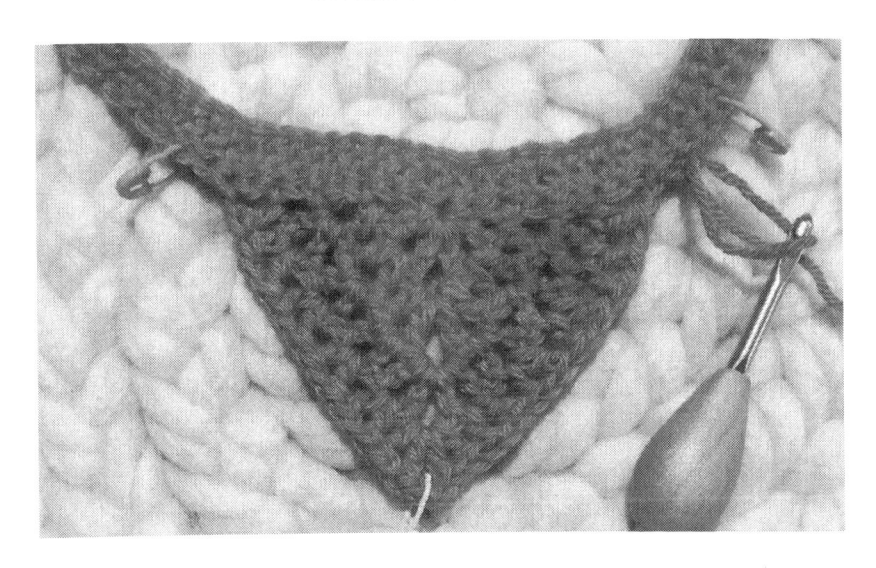

Row/Rnd 5: Ch 2, turn, (dc, ch 1, dc) in each ch-1 sp to marker, rm, (dc, ch 1, dc, ch 2, pm, dc, ch 1, dc) in ch-2 sp, (dc, ch 1, dc) in each ch-1 sp to marker, dc in marked st, ch 1, pm around ch just made, dc once more in marked st, rm, [skip 2, (dc, ch 1, dc) in next st] 20 times dc in marked st, ch 1, pm around ch just made, dc once more in marked st, rm, sl st to top of first dc made. {72 dc}

Row 6: Do not turn, 4 sc in next ch-1 sp, 3 sc in each ch-1 sp to marker, rm, (4 sc, ch 2, pm, 4 sc) in ch-2 sp, 3 sc in each ch-1 sp to marker, sc once more in same ch-1 sp, sl st in dc before marker, sl st in marked ch-1 sp, rm, pm in next st. {26 sc on each side}

Row 7: Turn, 2 sc in first sc, sc in each sc to marker, rm, (sc, ch 2, pm, sc) in ch-2 sp, sc in each sc until 1 sc remains, 2 sc in last sc, sl st in marked ch-1 sp, rm, sl st in next st, pm in next ch-1 sp. {28 sc on each side}

Row 8: Turn, 2 sc in first sc, sc in each sc to marker, rm, (sc, ch 2, pm, sc) in ch-2 sp, sc in each sc until 1 sc remains, 2 sc in last sc, sl st in marked st, rm, sl st in next st, sl st in next ch-1 sp, skip 1 dc, pm in next dc. {30 sc on each side}

Row 9: Ch 1, turn, (dc, ch 1, dc) in first sc, [skip 2, (dc, ch 1, dc) in next sc] until 2 sc before point marker, rm, (dc, ch 1, dc, ch 2, pm, dc, ch 1, dc) in ch-2 sp, [skip 2, (dc, ch 1, dc) in next sc] across side, ch 1, sl st in marked ch-1 sp, sl st in each of next 2 dc, skip ch-1 sp, pm in next dc. {22 dc on each side}

Row 10: Ch 1, turn, dc in first ch-1 sp of side, (dc, ch 1, dc) in each ch-1 sp to marker, rm, (dc, ch 1, dc, ch 2, pm, dc, ch 1, dc) in ch-2 sp, (dc, ch 1, dc) in each ch-1 sp across side until 1 ch-1 sp remains on side, dc in next ch-1, ch 1, sl st in marked dc, sl st in next ch-1 sp, sl st in next dc, skip next dc, pm in next ch-1 sp. {25 dc on each side}

Row 11: Ch 1, turn, (dc, ch 1, dc) in each ch-1 sp across side to marker, rm, (dc, ch 1, dc, ch 2, pm, dc, ch 1, dc) in ch-2 sp, (dc, ch 1, dc) in each ch-1 sp across side, ch 1, sl st in marked dc, rm, sl st in next dc, sl st in next ch-1 sp, pm in next ch-1 sp. {28 dc on each side}

Row 12: Ch 1, turn, dc in first ch-1 sp of side, (dc, ch 1, dc) in each ch-1 sp to marker, rm, (dc, ch 1, dc, ch 2, pm, dc, ch 1, dc) in ch-2 sp, (dc, ch 1, dc) in each ch-1 sp across side until 1 ch-1 sp remains on side, dc in next ch-1, ch 1, sl st in marked ch-1 sp, sl st in each of next 2 dc, pm in next ch-1 sp. {31 dc on each side}

Row/Rnd 13: Ch 2, turn, (dc, ch 1, dc) in each ch-1 sp across side to marker, rm, (dc, ch 1, dc, ch 2, pm, dc, ch 1, dc) in ch-2 sp, (dc, ch 1, dc) in each ch-1 sp across side, dc in marked ch-1 sp, ch 1, pm around ch just made, dc once more in marked ch-1 sp, rm, (dc, ch 1, dc) in each ch-1 sp to marker, dc in marked ch-1 sp, ch 1, pm around ch just made, dc once more in marked st, rm, sl st to top of first dc made. {96 dc}

Row 14: Repeat Row 6. {56 sc on each side}

Row 15: Repeat Row 7. {58 sc on each side}

Row 16: Repeat Row 8. {60 sc on each side}

Row 17: Repeat Row 9. {42 dc on each side}

Row 18: Repeat Row 10. {45 dc on each side}

Row 19: Repeat Row 11. {48 dc on each side}

Row 20: Repeat Row 12. {51 dc on each side}

Row/Rnd 21: Repeat Row/Rnd 13. {120 dc}

Row 22: Repeat Row 6. {86 sc on each side}

Row 23: Repeat Row 7. {88 sc on each side}

Row 24: Repeat Row 8. {90 sc on each side}

Row 25: Repeat Row 9, do not place last marker. {62 dc on each side}

Row 26: Ch 1, turn, dc in first ch-1 sp of side, (dc, ch 1, dc) in each ch-1 sp to marker, rm, (dc, ch 1, dc, ch 2, pm, dc, ch 1, dc) in ch-2 sp, (dc, ch 1, dc) in each ch-1 sp across side until 1 ch-1 sp remains on side, dc in next ch-1, ch 1, sl st in marked dc, rm, sl st in next ch-1 sp. {65 dc on each side}

Crochet Shawl Patterns

From this point on, continue working in rounds.

Rnd 27: Ch 4 (counts as first dc and ch-1 here and throughout), pm around ch just made, dc once more in same ch-1 sp, (dc, ch 1, dc) in each ch-1 sp to marker, rm, (dc, ch 1, dc, ch 2, pm, dc, ch 1, dc) in ch-2 sp, (dc, ch 1, dc) in each remaining ch-1 sp, sl st to 2nd ch of beginning ch-3. {140 dc}

Row 28: Sl st in marked ch-1 sp, rm, ch 4, pm around ch just made, dc once more in same ch-1 sp, (dc, ch 1, dc) in each ch-1 sp to marker, rm, (dc, ch 1, dc, ch 2, pm, dc, ch 1, dc) in ch-2 sp, (dc, ch 1, dc) in each remaining ch-1 sp, sl st to 2nd ch of beginning ch-3. {144 dc}

Rnd 29: Repeat Rnd 28. {148 dc}

Rnd 30: Sl st in marked ch-1 sp, rm, ch 1 (does not count as a st here or throughout), pm, 3 sc in same ch-1 sp, 3 sc in each ch-1 sp to marker, rm, (sc, ch 2, pm, sc) in ch-2 sp, 3 sc in each remaining ch-1 sp, sl st to top of beginning sc, rm. {224 sc}

Rnd 31: Ch 3 (counts as first dc), pm in last ch made, dc in each sc to marker, rm, (2 dc, ch 2, pm, 2 dc) in ch-2 sp, dc in each remaining sc, sl st to top of beginning ch 3, rm. {228 dc}

Rnd 32: Ch 1, pm, sc in each st to marker, rm, (sc, ch 2, pm, sc) in ch-2 sp, sc in each remaining st, sl st to top of beginning sc, rm. {230 sc}

Rnd 33: Sl st in each of next 2 sts, ch 5 (counts as first dc and ch-2 here and throughout), [skip 2, dc in next st, ch 2], to marker, rm, (dc, ch 2, pm, dc) in ch-2 sp, ch 2, dc in next st [ch 2, skip 2, dc in next st] until 3 sts remain, ch 2, sl st to 3rd ch of beginning ch 5. {79 dc}

Rnd 34: Ch 5, *dc in next dc, 2 dc in ch-2 sp, [dc in next dc, ch 2] 3 times; repeat from * until 2 dc remain before marker, dc in next dc, 2 dc in ch 2 sp, dc in next dc, ch 2, rm, (dc, ch 2, pm, dc) in ch-2 sp, ch 2, **dc in next dc, 2 dc in ch-2 sp, [dc in next dc, ch 2] 3 times; repeat from ** until 3 dc remain, dc in next dc, 2 dc in ch-2 sp, [dc in next dc, ch 2] 2 times, sl st to 3rd ch of beginning ch 5. {125 dc}

Rnd 35: Ch 5, dc in next dc, *ch 2, skip 2 dc, dc in next dc, [ch 2, dc in next dc] 3 times; repeat from * to 4 dc before marker, ch 2, skip 2 dc, [dc in next dc, ch 2] 2 times, rm, (dc, ch 2, pm, dc) in ch-2 sp, [ch 2, dc in next dc] 2 times, **ch 2, skip 2 dc, dc in next dc, [ch 2, dc in next dc] 3 times; repeat from * until 4 dc remain, ch 2, skip 2 dc, [dc in next dc, ch 2] 2 times, sl st to 3rd ch of beginning ch 5. {83 dc}

Rnd 36: Ch 5, [dc in next dc, ch 2] to marker, rm, (dc, ch 2, pm, dc) in ch-2 sp, [ch 2, dc in next dc] to end of rnd, ch 2, sl st to 3rd ch of beginning ch 5. {85 dc}

Rnd 37: Ch 4 (counts as first dc and ch 1), *(dc, ch 3, dc) in next dc, ch 1, dc in next dc, ch 1; repeat from * to marker, rm, (dc, ch 3, pm, dc) in ch-2 sp, **ch 1, dc in next dc, ch 1, (dc, ch 3, dc) in next dc; repeat from ** to end of rnd, ch 1, sl st to 3rd ch of beginning ch 4. {129 dc}

Rnd 38: Ch 1, sc in same dc, ch 1, *5 dc in ch-3 sp, ch 1, skip 1 dc, sc in next dc, ch 1; repeat from * to marker, rm, pm, 7 dc in ch-3 sp, ch 1, **skip 1 dc, sc in next dc, ch 1, 5 dc in ch-3 sp, ch 1; repeat from ** to end of round, sl st to top of beginning sc.

Rnd 39: Ch 1, *sl st in next dc, (ch 3, sl st in next dc) 4 times, ch 1, sl st in sc, ch 1, repeat from *to marker, rm, sl st in next dc, (ch 3, sl st in next dc) 3 times, (ch 3, sl st in first ch made) 3 times, sl st in same dc, (ch 3, sl st in next dc) 3 times, **ch 1, sl st in sc, ch 1, sl st in next dc, (ch 3, sl st in next dc) 4 times; repeat from ** to end of round, ch 1, sl st in first sl st of round.

Finish off then weave in ends.

Autumn Leaves Filet Crochet Shawl

Size: width - 20" (50 cm), length - 72" (180 cm)

Materials: Kauni (affiliate link) 8/2 Effektgarn 100% Wool sport weight yarn 660 yd (600 m)/150g, color EB - 2 skeins.

Hook: F (3.75 mm)

Gauge is not important

Abbreviations:

ch = chain

st(s) = stitch(es)

sl st = slip stitch

sc = single crochet

dc = double crochet

tr = treble crochet

dtr = double treble crochet

Pattern

Shawl

The shawl is worked in the filet crochet technique. The beginning and end of the shawl is done

using the Bruges tape technique.

Bruges tape

Chain 10.

Row 1: dc into the 7th chain from the hook. Dc 3 more times, turn

Row 2: ch 3 (counts as 1 dc), 3 dc over each of next 3 dc of the previous row, ch 6, turn.

Row 3: 4 dc into each of next 4 dc of the previous row, turn.

Repeat rows 2-3. Work 51 rows. Work ch 4 at the end of row 51 and start working the filet pattern along the Bruges tape, distributing stitches (and spaces) 2 sts per 1 row of the tape.

Alternatively, instead of the Bruges tape, chain 107 and work the first tr into the 6th st from the hook.

Open Mesh or Space

ch 2, skip 2, 1 tr

Solid Mesh or Block

3 tr (2 tr in ch 2 space or in each tr in row below, 1 tr)

Increase 1 Open Mesh at beginning of row

At the end of previous row, ch 9, turn and 1 tr in last tr of previous row.

Increase 1 Solid Mesh at beginning of row

At the end of previous row, ch 6, turn and 1 tr in 5th ch from hook, 1 tr in 6th ch from hook and

1 tr in last tr of previous row.

Lacet Stitch

Worked across two chart squares

ch 4, skip 2, 1 sc in next st, ch 4, skip 2 st, 1 tr in next st

Reverse Lacet Stitch

Worked across two chart squares

ch 2, 2 dtr tog (inserting hook in same place as prev tr, then in next tr), ch 2, 1 tr in the same place as last insertion.

The shawl is worked as follows: 1 solid mesh, (lacet or reverse laset st over 2 squares, 3 solid meshes) 4 times, (the last solid mesh column has only 2 solid meshes), leaf border.

Work the shawl following the diagram to desired length. End with the Bruges tape:

Chain 10.

Row 1: dc into the 7th chain from the hook. Dc 3 more times, sl st to filet mesh, turn

Row 2: ch 3 (counts as 1 dc), sl st to filet mesh, 3 dc over the each of next 3 dc of the previous row, ch 6, turn.

Row 3: 4 dc into the each of next 4 dc of the previous row, sl st to filet mesh, turn.

Repeat rows 2-3. Work 51 rows. Tie off.

Finishing

Block the shawl.

Any Season Asymmetrical Shawlette

Materials

1 hank fingering weight yarn, approx. 445 yds (shown here in Manos del Uruguay Alegria in the colorway A2545 Pewter), or more for larger shawl

US E / 3.5 mm crochet hook

scissors and needle

Finished size as written measures approx. 34.5" x 41" x 26.5", but is easily customization to the size you desire.

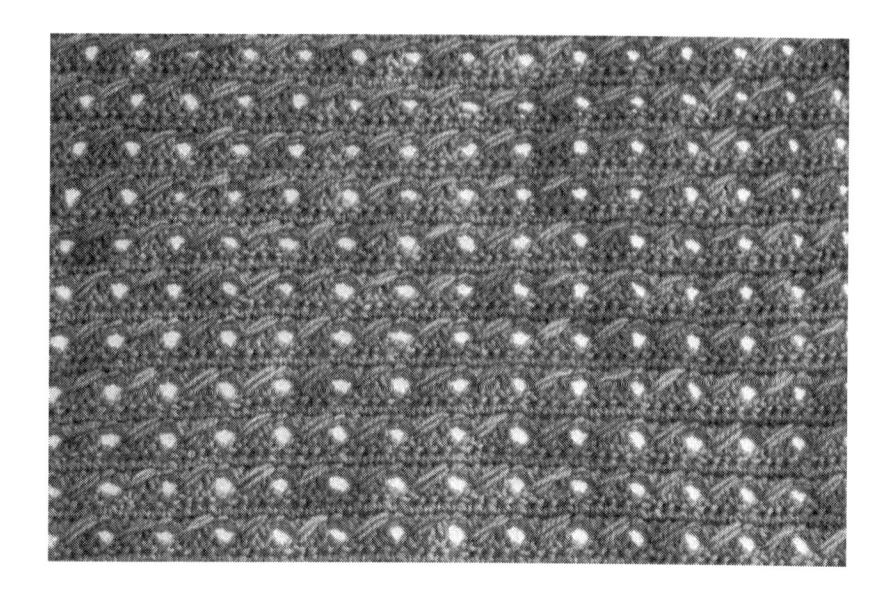

Pattern

Ch 7.

Row 1: Work 1 sc in second ch from hook and each ch across, turn – 6 sts.

Row 2: Ch 1 (does not count as st here and throughout), work 1 sc in each st across, turn – 6 sts.

Row 3: Ch 3 (counts as dc here and throughout), skip next st, work 1 dc in each of the next 3 sts, work 1 dc back across the sts just made and into the skipped st, work 1 dc in last st, turn – 6 sts.

Row 4: Ch 1, work 2 sc in each of the next 3 sts, 1 sc in next, 2 sc in next, 1 sc in last, turn – 10 sts.

Row 5: Ch 3, *skip next st, work 1 dc in each of the next 3 sts, work 1 dc back across the sts just made and into the skipped st, repeat from *, work 1 dc in last st, turn – 10 sts.

Row 6: Ch 1, work 1 sc in each st across, turn – 10 sts.

Row 7: Ch 3, *skip next st, work 1 dc in each of the next 3 sts, work 1 dc back across the sts just made and into the skipped st, repeat from * across, work 1 dc in last st, turn – 10 sts.

Row 8: Ch 1, *work 2 sc in next st, 1 sc in next, rep from * 3 more times, work 1 sc in each of the remaining sts, turn – 14 sts.

Row 9: Ch 3, *skip next st, work 1 dc in each of the next 3 sts, work 1 dc back across the sts just made and into the skipped st, repeat from * across, work 1 dc in last st, turn – 14 sts.

Row 10: Ch 1, work 1 sc in each st across, turn – 14 sts.

Rows 11 through 110: Repeat Rows 7 through 10 until Row 110 or until desired length is reached, increasing by 4 sts with each repeat – 118 sts.

Weave in ends and block if desired.

My Story Shawl

Materials

Scheepjes Whirl Pistachi Oh So Nice (761) – 4 ply/220 g/1000 meters (60% cotton/40% acrylic) – available from WoolWarehouse and Deramores (Internationally), as well as other Scheepjes retailers.

3.25 mm crochet hook

Abbreviations

Ch – Chain

Dc – Double crochet

Sl St – Slip stitch

St – Stitch

() – Repeat instructions between parentheses the number of times specified. Also used to indicate stitches to be worked into the same stitch/space.

Gauge

Following the pattern: 15 dc + 14 ch-1 spaces (width) and 13 rows (height) per 10 cm (4") square – unblocked.

Gauge is not massively important with this pattern.

Size

192 cm wide by 64 cm high (75" x 25") – unblocked.

Notes

If you need help with the magic ring, please see THIS TUTORIAL. I still advise you to work your yarn ends away VERY thoroughly when using the magic ring.

The picot edge of this shawl is created as you go. Your work will be asymmetric at the end of every row. Each row will have a picot at the start, but not at the end. This will be fixed at the start of each subsequent row.

Crochet Shawl Patterns

Chart

Crochet Shawl Patterns

Pattern

Row 1

Working into a Magic Ring:

Ch 6 and sl st into the fourth chain from the hook (indicated with an arrow in Photo 1 and illustrated in Photo 2). This counts as your first dc and picot throughout. Make 2 dc. (Ch 3, 3 dc) twice. Close the magic ring and turn. {9 dc, 1 picot, and 2 ch-3 spaces}

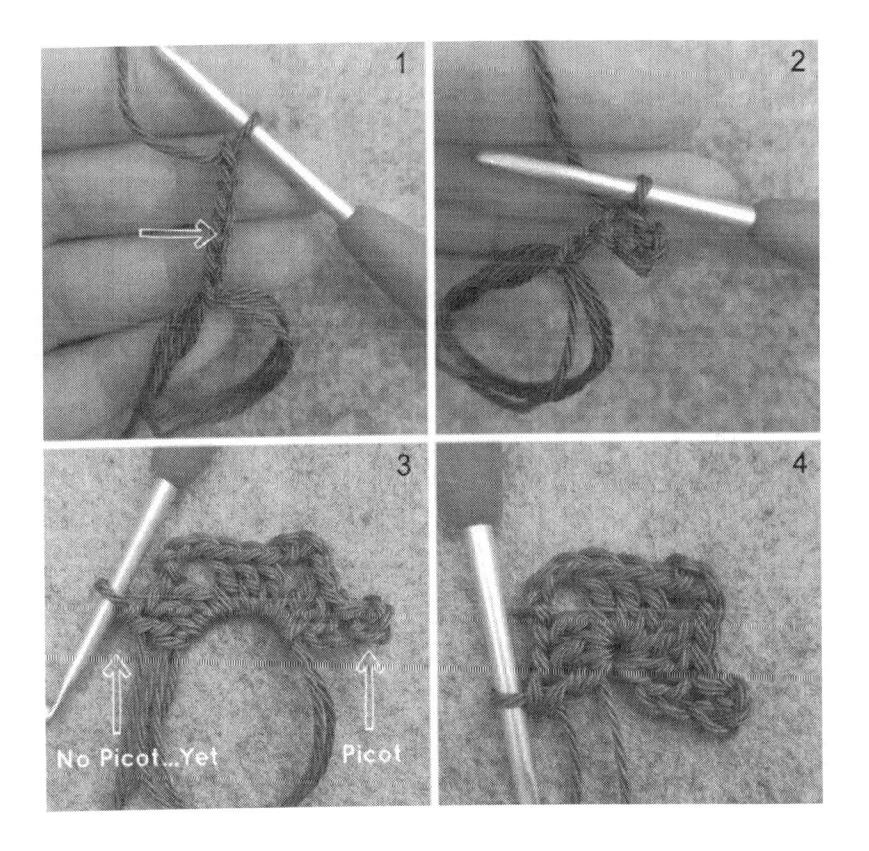

Row 2

Ch 3, sl st in the dc at the base of the ch-3 to form a picot (indicated with an arrow in Photo 1 and illustrated in Photo 2). Sl st in the next 2 dc and in the ch-3 space (Photo 3). Ch 6 and sl st into the fourth chain from the hook. (2 dc, ch 3, 3 dc) into the same ch-3 space (Photo 4). Ch 1, skip the next st and dc in the next st. Ch 1 and skip the last st. (3 dc, ch 3, 3 dc) in the next ch-3 space (Photo 5). Turn. {13 dc, 1 picot, 2 ch-1 spaces, and 2 ch-3 spaces}

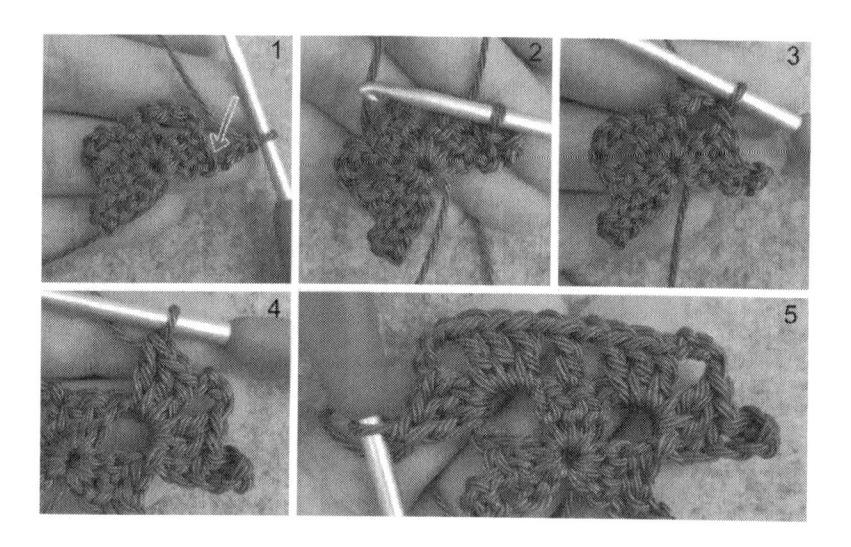

Row 3

Ch 3, sl st in the dc at the base of the ch-3 to form a picot. Sl st in the next 2 dc and in the ch-3 space. Ch 6 and sl st into the fourth chain from the hook, (2 dc, ch 3, 3 dc) into the same ch-3 space. Ch 1, skip the next st and dc in the next st. (Ch 1, dc in the next ch-1 space) until you have worked into each ch-1 space. Ch 1, skip the next st and dc in the next st. Ch 1 and skip the last st. (3 dc, ch 3, 3 dc) in the next ch-3 space. Turn. {16 dc, 1 picot, 5 ch-1 spaces, and 2 ch-3 spaces}

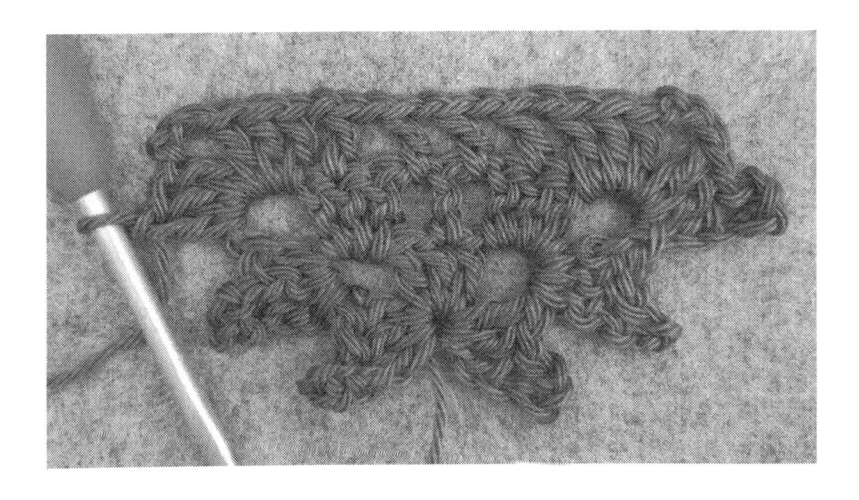

Rows 4 to Forever (see Note below)

Repeat Row 3. Each repeat will have 3 more dc and 3 more ch-1 spaces than the previous repeat.

Note

For the example shawl, Jenny ended up making 86 rows in total. Depending on your tension, you might have to make more or fewer rows. Just keep repeating Row 3 until you don't have enough yarn to make another repeat, or until your shawl is as large as you want it to be, then finish off as instructed below.

Finishing Off

When you have made your last row, ch 3 and sl st in the dc at the base of the ch-3 to form a picot, remembering to turn before you do so. Fasten off and work away your ends.

Halo Shawl

Materials

Audine Wools by Knitcrate, 50% Alpaca/30% Merino/20% Nylon, 100g/215m/236yds

2 skeins in Blush

5mm Crochet Hook (or size that fits your tension)

You can use any DK weight yarn to achieve a similar effect

Measurements

Crochet Shawl Patterns

76in (cm) length x 29in (cm) depth – after blocking laid flat without tassels

Notes

Shawl is a triangle creating a wing span with a width of approx. 76"

The main body is worked in one piece from bottom-up, increasing on each side until a shallow wide triangle is made.

The shawl can be made larger or smaller by working more or fewer pattern repeats. This will alter the amount of yarn required.

You can use any weight yarn and matching hook to achieve a similar effect. Go up a hook size if you crochet on the tight side

Includes written instructions. Pattern written in US and UK crochet terms

Blocking is important as it will help open up the stitches of the pattern

Gauge is not important

Abbreviations

US Crochet Terms

Dc   double crochet

Tr   treble crochet

Ch   chain

Rep	repeat
Beg	beginning
Sp	space
T-ch	turning chain

UK Crochet Terms

Tc	treble crochet
Dtr	double treble crochet
Ch	chain
Rep	repeat
Beg	beginning
Sp	space
T-ch	turning chain

Video

Halo Shawl Video

×

Pattern (US Terms)

Row 1: Using 5mm hook ch5 (counts as beg ch and 1tr), [1dc, ch2, 1dc, 1tr] in 5th ch from hook, turn – 2tr, 2dc

Row 2: Ch4 (counts as 1tr here and throughout), [1dc, ch2, 1dc] in 1st st, 1sc in ch-2 sp, [1dc, ch2, 1dc, 1tr] in last st (t-ch), turn – 2tr, 4dc, 1sc

Row 3: Ch4, [1dc, ch2, 1dc] in 1st st, 1sc in next ch-2 sp, [1dc, ch2, 1dc] in next sc, 1sc in next ch-2 sp, [1dc, ch2, 1dc, 1tr] in last st (t-ch), turn – 2tr, 6dc, 2sc

Row 4: Ch4, [1dc, ch2, 1dc] in 1st st, 1sc in next ch-2 sp, * [1dc, ch2, 1dc] in next sc, 1sc in next ch-2 sp; rep from * across ending with [1dc, ch2, 1dc, 1tr] in last st (t-ch), turn.

Rows 5 – 46: Repeat row 4

I did a total of 46 rows but you may make less or more, depending on size you want/how much yarn you have!

You will work one last row to straighten the top of your shawl

Final Row: Working across the top edge, ch4, sl st into 1st ch-2 sp, * ch4, sl st into next ch-2 sp; rep from * across, ch4, sl st into top of last st. And you are done!

Pattern (UK Terms)

Row 1: Using 5mm hook ch5 (counts as beg ch and 1dtr), [1tr, ch2, 1tr, 1dtr] in 5th ch from hook, turn – 2dtr, 2tr

Row 2: Ch4 (counts as 1dtr here and throughout), [1tr, ch2, 1tr] in 1st st, 1dc in ch-2 sp, [1tr, ch2, 1tr, 1dtr] in last st (t-ch), turn – 2dtr, 4tr, 1dc

Row 3: Ch4, [1tr, ch2, 1tr] in 1st st, 1dc in next ch-2 sp, [1tr, ch2, 1tr] in next dc, 1dc in next ch-2 sp, [1tr, ch2, 1tr, 1dtr] in last st (t-ch), turn – 2dtr, 6tr, 2dc

Row 4: Ch4, [1tr, ch2, 1tr] in 1st st, 1dc in next ch-2 sp, * [1tr, ch2, 1tr] in next dc, 1dc in next ch-2 sp; rep from * across ending with [1tr, ch2, 1tr, 1dtr] in last st (t-ch), turn.

Rows 5 – 46: Repeat row 4

I did a total of 46 rows but you may make less or more, depending on size you want/how much yarn you have!

You will work one last row to straighten the top of your shawl.

Final Row: Working across the top edge, ch4, sl st into 1st ch-2 sp, * ch4, sl st into next ch-2 sp; rep from * across, ch4, sl st into top of last st. And you are done!

Finishing

Weave in all loose ends. Lay project out to finished size and pull gently into shape. Pin in place and spray lightly with water and leave to dry. You can wet block shawl if desired – check your yarn fiber instructions. Add tassels if you wish.

Tassel Instructions

Make 3 tassels as follows: Using a book approx. 4-6" in width, cut a 12" length of yarn and lay across top of book – this will be used to tie top of tassel. Wrap yarn around book about 16 – 20 times (depending on thickness required). Using the 12" tie, knot top of tassel tightly. Cut tassel at opposite end. Wrap another length of yarn around tassel 1" from top approx. 5 times and knot ends together. Trim if needed and sew securely to 3 corners of shawl.

Winter Shawl

Materials:

Hook: I/9/5.5mm

Yarn: Cascade 220 – 3 skeins silver grey, 1 skein summer sky

Tools: Scissors, tapestry needle

ABBREVIATIONS:

st = stitch

ch = chain

hhdc= herringbone half double crochet

hdc=half double crochet

dc=double crochet

sk=skip

sp=space

SPECIAL INFORMATION: Herringbone half double crochet:

Yo, insert hook in indicated st, pull up a loop through st and first loop on hook. Yo again and pull through the last two loops on the hook.

FINISHED SIZE: 70" Wide, 36" long

Gauge: 8 rows x 12 st = 4"

Pattern

Begin using Silver Gray and make a magic ring

Row 1: Ch 3 (counts as first dc), Make 3 more dc and ch 2. Make 4 more dc and pull to tighten (8 dc)

Row 2: Ch 3, dc in the first st. Dc in each st to ch-2 sp, (2 dc, ch 2, 2 dc) in the ch-2 sp, dc in each st across to last st, 2 dc into the last st, turn. (14 dc)

Rows 3-9: Repeat row 2. (56 dc at the end of row 9)

Row 10: Ch 3, dc in the first st. *ch 1, sk 1 st, dc into next st*, rep between * to dc before to ch-2 sp, ch 1, sk next dc, (2 dc, ch 2, 2 dc) in the ch-2 sp. Repeat between * across to last 2 sts, ch 1, sk 1 st, 2 dc in last st, turn. (34 dc, 28 ch-1 sp)

Row 11: Ch 3, dc into the first st. Dc in each st and ch-1 sp to ch-2 sp, (2 dc, ch 2, 2 dc) in the ch-2 sp, dc in each st and ch-1 sp across to last st, 2 dc into the last st, turn. (68 dc)

Row 12-14: Repeat row 2. (86 dc at row 14)

Row 15: Ch 3, dc in the first st. Dc in next st, *ch 1, sk 1 st, dc into next st*, rep between * to dc before to ch-2 sp, ch 1, sk next dc, (2 dc, ch 2, 2 dc) in the ch-2 sp. Repeat between * across to last st, 2 dc in last st, turn. (50 dc, 42 ch-1 sps)

Row 16: Ch 3, dc into the first st. Dc in each st and ch-1 sp to ch-2 sp, (2 dc, ch 2, 2 dc) in the ch-2 sp, dc in each st and ch-1 sp across to last st, 2 dc into the last st, turn. (98 dc)

Rows 17-19: Repeat row 2. (116 at row 19)

Rows 20-39: Repeat rows 10-19 three times. (296 dc at the end of row 39). At end of last row, fasten off.

Row 41: With summer sky, 2 hhdc in the first st, hhdc in each st to the ch-2 sp. (2 hhdc, ch 2, 2 hhdc) in ch-2 sp. Hhdc in each st to last st, making 2 hhdc in the last sp, turn. (302 hhdc)

Rows 42-48: Repeat row 41. (344 hhdc at end of row 48) Break yarn, weave in all ends.

Grab a hook and make this unique shawl pattern for a loved one. You can't go wrong and you'll pick up some new skills along the way. This shawl wrap is so easy to construct and fun too. It's perfect for cold weather thanks to the 100% wool yarn it's make with.

Pop Of Color Shawl

Materials

Hook: I/9/5.5mm

Yarn: Cascade 220 Superwash Merino — 3 skeins doeskin heather (approx. 580 yards); 2 skeins sugar coral (approx. 310 yards)

Tools: Tapestry Needle & Scissors

ABBREVIATIONS:

st = stitch

ch = chain

sc = single crochet

dc = double crochet

sk = skip

sp = space

SPECIAL INFORMATION:

FINISHED SIZE: 65" wide, 40" long

Gauge: 12 dc x 8 rows = 4"

Pattern:

Row 1: Using doeskin, make a magic ring. Ch 3 (counts as first dc here and throughout), 3 dc in ring, ch 2, 4 dc in ring, turn. Pull to tighten (8 dc)

Row 2: Ch 3, dc in the first st. Dc in each st to the ch-2 sp. (2 dc, ch 2, 2 dc) in ch-2 sp. Dc in each st to last st, 2 dc in the last st, turn. (14 dc)

Rows 3-39: Repeat row 2. At end of last row, fasten off.(Last row will have 236 dc)

Row 40: With sugar coral, ch 2 (counts as sc and ch-1), sc in the 2nd st. *ch 1, sk 1 st, sc in the next st*, repeat between * across to ch-2 sp, ch 1, (sc, ch 2, sc) in ch-2 sp, ch 1, sc into the first st after the ch-2 sp, rep between * across, to last st, ch 1, sc in last st, turn. (120 ch-1 sps, 122 sc)

Row 41: Ch 2, sc into the first ch-1 sp *ch 1, sk 1 sc, sc in the next ch-1 sp*, repeat between * across to ch-2 sp, ch 1, (sc, ch 2, sc) in ch-2 sp, ch 1, sc into the first ch-1 sp after the ch-2 sp, rep between * across ending with (sc, ch 1, sc) in last ch-2, turn. (122 ch-1 sps, 124 sc)

Row 42-49: Repeat row 41.

Fasten off and weave in all ends.

Crochet Shawl Patterns

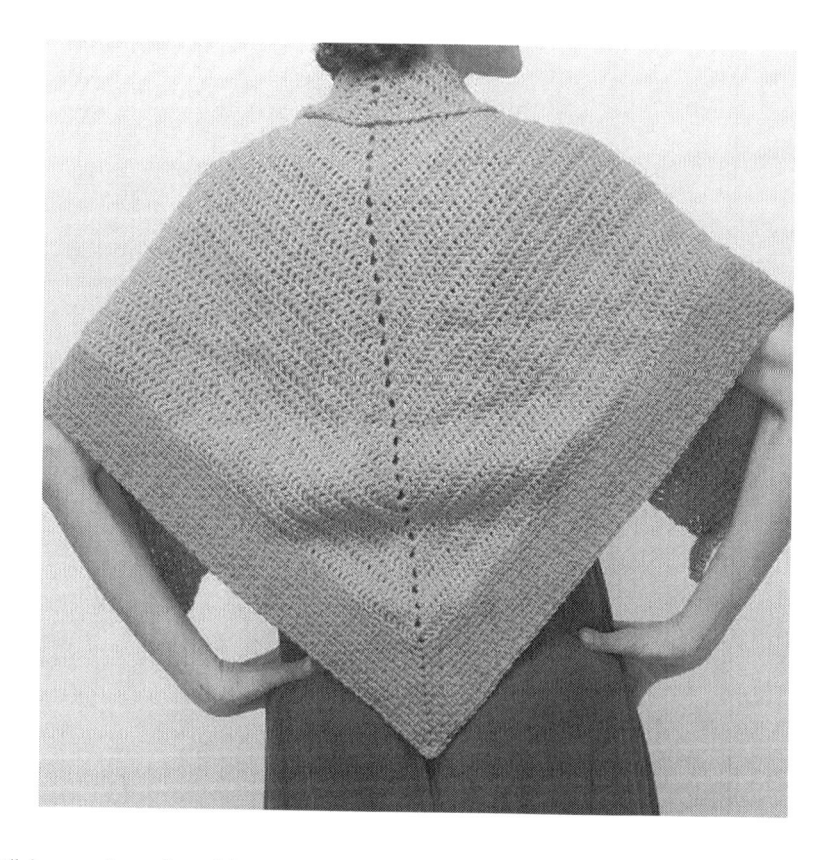

This crochet shawl is easy to make and will teach you how to crochet a triangle. I love projects that I can learn new skills from and this crochet shawl pattern is just that. Pick up your hook and make yourself a pop of color shawl wrap today.

April Showers Shawl

Materials

3.5 skeins of I Love This Yarn! Stonewash in Mint Lace — 5 oz/ 142 g — 252 yds/230 m (only 3 skeins if you don't want the fringe)

Or any size 4 medium weight yarn

I/9 (5.25 mm) hook — My favorite hooks! I use them daily!

Tapestry needle

Measuring tape to determine size needed

Finished Size Approximately:

60" Width x 38" Length (without fringe)

Gauge:

16 double crochet stitches and 7 rows in a 4" (10cm) square.

Special Stitches:

Triple (Treble) Crochet

YO twice, insert hook into stitch, YO and draw back through. YO and draw through two loops, YO and draw through 2 loops, YO and draw through two loops.

Abbreviations:

YO – yarn over

FC – foundation chain (beginning chain)

sc – single crochet

dc – double crochet

tc – triple (treble) crochet

sl st – slip stitch

ch(s) – chain(s)

st(s) – stitch(es)

Notes:

- One side of the single crochet border is worked in as you build the main body of your shawl. When you go to add a border at the end, you will only crochet your single crochet stitches around 2 sides.

- This example April Showers shawl measures 60" across. If you would like a larger or smaller shawl, use this chart at the end of the pattern.
- For sizing, stand with arms spread wide. Measure from finger tip to finger tip (or a few inches longer if you like your shawls over-sized) and find the closest measurement from the chart below. If your measurement is in between, I recommend you size up.

*** American crochet terms used throughout.

Pattern:

FC: Ch 242

Row 1: In 2nd ch from hook, sc. *Ch 1, skip 4 chs. In next ch, (tc, ch 2, tc, ch 2, tc, ch 2, tc, ch 2, tc). Ch 1, skip 4 chs, sc in next ch.* Repeat from * to * across. Turn.

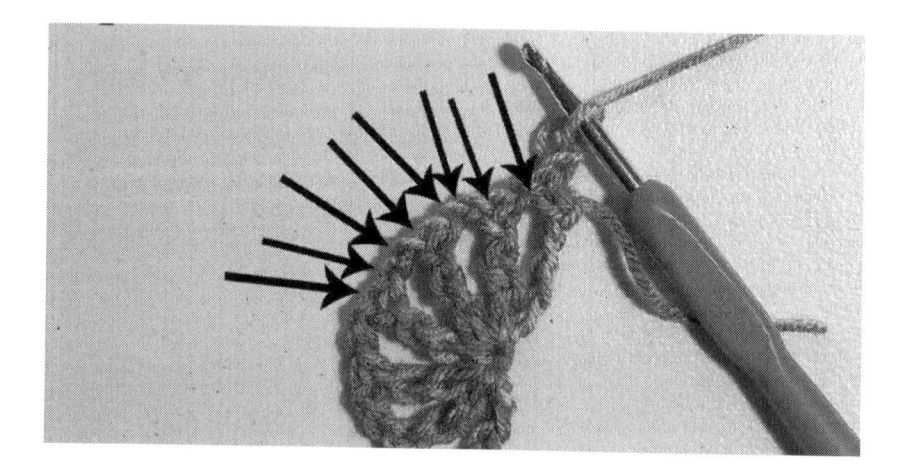

Row 2: Ch 1, sc in next ch-1 space. Sc in top of tc from previous row. *2 sc in ch-2 space, sc in tc* Repeat from * to * once more. Sc in next tc. (See photo below) **Ch 3, skip 1st ch-2 space. In next ch-2 space, dc. Ch 2, skip the next two ch-1 spaces, dc in next ch-2 space. Ch 3. Skip next ch-2 space, sc in the top of the next tc from the previous row (middle spike of the 5)** Repeat from ** to ** across. Turn.

Crochet Shawl Patterns

This photo shows the completed single crochets from the above photo.

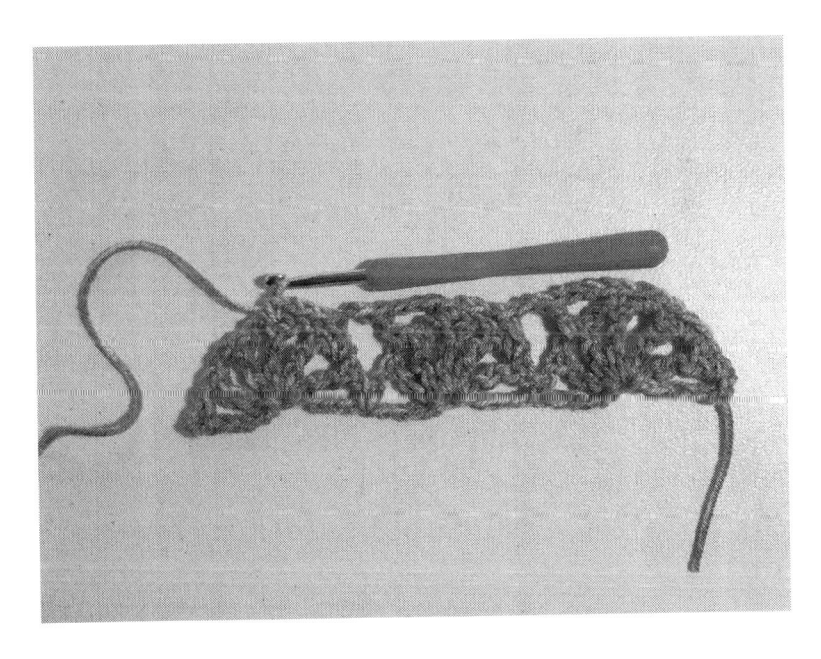

Leave the rest of the stitches unworked. This creates the natural decrease. Always stop your row 2 repeat at the middle tc of the last half circle.

Row 3: Ch 1, sc in same st ch-1 comes out of. *Ch 1. Skip the ch-3 space. In next ch-2 space, (tc, ch 2, tc, ch 2, tc, ch 2, tc, ch 2, tc). Ch 1, skip the ch-3 space, sc in next st* Repeat from * to * across. Turn.

Note: At the end of every Row 3 repeat, after you make your final sc, sl st in the next st. This will keep your border of single crochets solid.

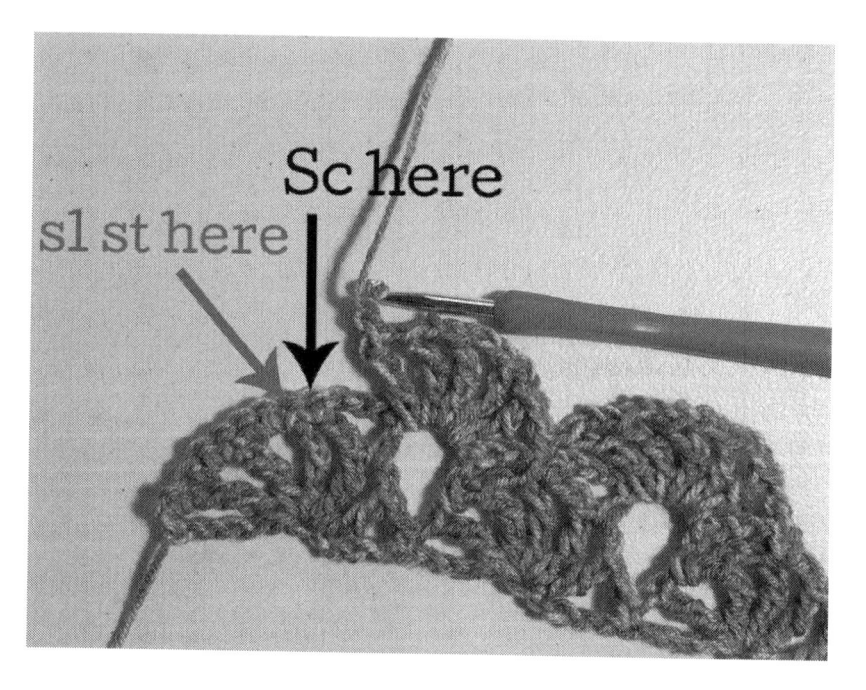

Alternate Row 2 and Row 3 for the pattern. The number of rows you need to work are included in the graph below.

Don't finish off after last row.

Border

One side of the shawl already has a row of single crochets. You will ch 1 after your last row and turn. Work single crochets evenly around the bottom tip of the shawl and up the side that doesn't already have a border. At the top corner, (sc, ch 3, sc) all in the same space. Continue single crocheting evenly along the top of the shawl. At the next corner, (sc, ch 3, sc) and slip stitch in the first single crochet of the preexisting border.

Finish off. Weave in ends.

Crochet Triangle Shawl

Materials

2 skeins Red Heart Super Saver Ombre (Finished shawl pictured in Deep Teal; tutorial shawl pictured in Spearmint)

5.5mm crochet hook

Sharp scissors (You want really sharp scissors for your tassels! So be careful!)

Crochet Shawl Patterns

3" by 4.5" cut piece of cardboard or sturdy posterboard

Yarn needle

Key

ch – chain

dc – double crochet

sk – skip

sl st – slip stitch

sp – space

st – stitch

Gauge

4 inches is equal to approximately 12 dc by 7 rows

Finished Measurement

One size fits all

Approximately 63 inches wide (along top edge) with a 39 inch depth (from middle top edge to triangular peak)

Sizing notes

For a larger size, purchase additional skeins and complete repeats until you reach your your desired fit.

For a smaller size, make less repeats than what the pattern calls for.

Make repeats until you reach your desired fit.

Note

The starting ch 3 of each row will count as a stitch, unless otherwise noted.

Pattern

Row 1: In magic ring, ch 3 (counts as a dc) and make 5 dc, ch 2, 6 dc; turn (12)

You will be working back and forth in rows.

Row 2: Ch 3, dc in same st as ch 3, dc in each st up to ch 2 sp, make 2 dc, ch 2, 2 dc in ch sp, dc to end making 2 dc in the 3rd ch of the ch 3 from previous row; turn (18)

Rows 3 – 5: Repeat Row 2. (Please note that as you crochet each row, the stitch count will increase. So after completing Row 3, you will end with 24 stitches, and so on.)

Row 6: Ch 3, dc in same st as ch 3, ch 1, sk a st, *dc, ch1, sk a st; repeat from * until you reach ch 2 sp (you should end w/ a ch 1, sk a stitch when you arrive at the ch 2 sp); 2 dc, ch 2, 2 dc in ch 2 sp, ch 1, sk a st, * dc, ch 1, sk a st; repeat from * to end of row, make 2 dc in 3rd ch of ch 3 from previous row; turn.

Row 7: Ch 3, dc in same st as ch 3, dc in ch sp, dc in dc, continue making dc's in each stitch and ch 1 sp until you reach the center ch 2 sp, 2 dc, ch 2, 2 dc in ch 2 sp, continue making dc's until end of row,

Crochet Shawl Patterns

making 2 dc's in the 3rd ch of the ch 3 from previous row; turn.

Rows 8 – 11: Repeat Row 2

Row 12: Repeat Row 6

Repeat Repeat Rows 7 – 12, six times.

Border Round

Lay piece flat in front of you with whichever side you would like to be the front. Position so that the flat edge is at the top, and the triangular portion is towards the bottom.

Start at the top right corner. (If you are not already at the top right corner, cut yarn and secure. Attach yarn at top right corner.)

Ch 1, (ch 1 does not count as st) make 3 sc in corner stitch that you are currently in and sc across top edge, making 2 sc per row; in top center stitch make 1 dc; make 3 sc in second corner. I had approximately 187 stitches (not counting my corners) along my top edge – this doesn't have to perfect! Sc in each st along triangular bottom, making 3 sc in the center ch 2 sp. Join with 1st sc of round using a sl st.

Cut yarn, weave in ends.

Spring Shawl

Materials

Lion Brand Vanna's Choice in Linen (2 skeins), Pink, Sage, Dusty Purple, Dusty Blue

6.0 mm hook

Yarn needle

Crochet Shawl Patterns

Scissors

Level

Easy+ -you must be very familiar with basic crochet stitches

Pattern notes & stitches to know

Ch – chain

Sl st – slip stitch

Dc – double crochet

Puff stitch – *yarn over, insert hook into stitch, pull up a loop* repeat 2 more times, yarn over, pull through all loops on hook

Approximate Finished Size (not including tassels):

Width: 55" across the top at the widest part

Length: 32" down the middle at the longest part

Pattern

Ch 3 at beginning of each round counts as dc

Start with Linen

Ch 4, sl st to the first ch to form a ring

Row 1: ch 3, (2 dc, ch 2, 3 dc) into ring

Row 2: Ch 3, turn, dc in same stitch and in next 2, (2 dc, ch 2, 2 dc) in ch 2 space, dc in next 2 stitches, 2 dc in last stitch

Row 3: ch 3, turn, dc in same stitch and in next 5, (2 dc, ch 2, 2 dc) in ch 2 space, dc in next 5, 2 dc in last stitch

Row 4: ch 3, turn, dc in same stitch and across to ch 2 space, (2 dc, ch 2, 2 dc) in ch 2 space, dc in each stitch to the last stitch, 2 dc in last stitch

Repeat row 4 to row 19

Change to Pink

Row 20: repeat row 4

Row 21: ch 4 (counts as dc + ch 1), turn, dc in same stitch, *ch 1, skip one stitch, puff stitch in next* repeat from * to * across to ch 2 space, (puff stitch, ch 2, puff stitch) all in ch 2 space, repeat from * to * across to last stitch, (dc, ch 1, dc) all in last stitch

Row 22: ch 3, turn, dc in same stitch, dc in each puff stitch and ch 1 space across to ch 2 space, (2 dc, ch 2, 2 dc) all in ch 2 space, dc in each puff stitch and ch 1 space across to the last stitch, 2 dc in last stitch

Change to Linen

Row 23: repeat row 4

Change to Sage

Row 24: repeat row 4

Row 25: ch 4 (counts as dc + ch 1), turn, dc in same stitch, *ch 1, skip one stitch, puff stitch in next* repeat from * to * across to ch 2 space, (puff stitch, ch 2, puff stitch) all in ch 2 space, repeat from * to * across to last stitch, (dc, ch 1, dc) all in last stitch

Row 26: ch 3, turn, dc in same stitch, dc in each puff stitch and ch 1 space across to ch 2 space, (2 dc, ch 2, 2 dc) all in ch 2 space, dc in each puff stitch and ch 1 space across to the last stitch, 2 dc in last stitch

Change to Linen

Row 27: repeat row 4

Change to Dusty Purple

Row 28: repeat row 4

Row 29: ch 4 (counts as dc + ch 1), turn, dc in same stitch, *ch 1, skip one stitch, puff stitch in next* repeat from * to * across to ch 2 space, (puff stitch, ch 2, puff stitch) all in ch 2 space, repeat from * to * across to last stitch, (dc, ch 1, dc) all in last stitch

Row 30: ch 3, turn, dc in same stitch, dc in each puff stitch and ch 1 space across to ch 2 space, (2 dc, ch 2, 2 dc) all in ch 2 space, dc in each puff stitch and ch 1 space across to the last stitch, 2 dc in last stitch

Change to Linen

Row 31: repeat row 4

Change to Dusty Blue

Row 32: repeat row 4

Row 33: ch 4 (counts as dc + ch 1), turn, dc in same stitch, *ch 1, skip one stitch, puff stitch in next* repeat from * to * across to ch 2 space, (puff stitch, ch 2, puff stitch) all in ch 2 space, repeat from * to * across to last stitch, (dc, ch 1, dc) all in last stitch

Row 34: ch 3, turn, dc in same stitch, dc in each puff stitch and ch 1 space across to ch 2 space, (2 dc, ch 2, 2 dc) all in ch 2 space, dc in each puff stitch and ch 1 space across to the last stitch, 2 dc in last stitch

Change to Linen

Row 35: repeat row 4

Fasten off, weave in all the ends.

Made in the USA
Middletown, DE
10 August 2020